Contact

NICHOLAS
KIRSTEN
HOUSHU

2022 AT A GLANCE

JANUARY 2022

S	M	T	W	T	F	S
						1
2	3	4	5	6	7	8
9	10	11	12	13	14	15
16	17	18	19	20	21	22
23	24	25	26	27	28	29
30	31					

FEBRUARY 2022

S	M	T	W	T	F	S
		1	2	3	4	5
6	7	8	9	10	11	12
13	14	15	16	17	18	19
20	21	22	23	24	25	26
27	28					

MARCH 2022

S	M	T	W	T	F	S
		1	2	3	4	5
6	7	8	9	10	11	12
13	14	15	16	17	18	19
20	21	22	23	24	25	26
27	28	29	30	31		

APRIL 2022

S	M	T	W	T	F	S
					1	2
3	4	5	6	7	8	9
10	11	12	13	14	15	16
17	18	19	20	21	22	23
24	25	26	27	28	29	30

MAY 2022

S	M	T	W	T	F	S
1	2	3	4	5	6	7
8	9	10	11	12	13	14
15	16	17	18	19	20	21
22	23	24	25	26	27	28
29	30	31				

JUNE 2022

S	M	T	W	T	F	S
			1	2	3	4
5	6	7	8	9	10	11
12	13	14	15	16	17	18
19	20	21	22	23	24	25
26	27	28	29	30		

JULY 2022

S	M	T	W	T	F	S
					1	2
3	4	5	6	7	8	9
10	11	12	13	14	15	16
17	18	19	20	21	22	23
24	25	26	27	28	29	30
31						

AUGUST 2022

S	M	T	W	T	F	S
	1	2	3	4	5	6
7	8	9	10	11	12	13
14	15	16	17	18	19	20
21	22	23	24	25	26	27
28	29	30	31			

SEPTEMBER 2022

S	M	T	W	T	F	S
				1	2	3
4	5	6	7	8	9	10
11	12	13	14	15	16	17
18	19	20	21	22	23	24
25	26	27	28	29	30	

OCTOBER 2022

S	M	T	W	T	F	S
						1
2	3	4	5	6	7	8
9	10	11	12	13	14	15
16	17	18	19	20	21	22
23	24	25	26	27	28	29
30	31					

NOVEMBER 2022

S	M	T	W	T	F	S
		1	2	3	4	5
6	7	8	9	10	11	12
13	14	15	16	17	18	19
20	21	22	23	24	25	26
27	28	29	30			

DECEMBER 2022

S	M	T	W	T	F	S
				1	2	3
4	5	6	7	8	9	10
11	12	13	14	15	16	17
18	19	20	21	22	23	24
25	26	27	28	29	30	31

2023 AT A GLANCE

JANUARY 2023

S	M	T	W	T	F	S
1	2	3	4	5	6	7
8	9	10	11	12	13	14
15	16	17	18	19	20	21
22	23	24	25	26	27	28
29	30	31				

FEBRUARY 2023

S	M	T	W	T	F	S
			1	2	3	4
5	6	7	8	9	10	11
12	13	14	15	16	17	18
19	20	21	22	23	24	25
26	27	28				

MARCH 2023

S	M	T	W	T	F	S
			1	2	3	4
5	6	7	8	9	10	11
12	13	14	15	16	17	18
19	20	21	22	23	24	25
26	27	28	29	30	31	

APRIL 2023

S	M	T	W	T	F	S
						1
2	3	4	5	6	7	8
9	10	11	12	13	14	15
16	17	18	19	20	21	22
23	24	25	26	27	28	29
30						

MAY 2023

S	M	T	W	T	F	S
	1	2	3	4	5	6
7	8	9	10	11	12	13
14	15	16	17	18	19	20
21	22	23	24	25	26	27
28	29	30	31			

JUNE 2023

S	M	T	W	T	F	S
				1	2	3
4	5	6	7	8	9	10
11	12	13	14	15	16	17
18	19	20	21	22	23	24
25	26	27	28	29	30	

JULY 2023

S	M	T	W	T	F	S
						1
2	3	4	5	6	7	8
9	10	11	12	13	14	15
16	17	18	19	20	21	22
23	24	25	26	27	28	29
30	31					

AUGUST 2023

S	M	T	W	T	F	S
		1	2	3	4	5
6	7	8	9	10	11	12
13	14	15	16	17	18	19
20	21	22	23	24	25	26
27	28	29	30	31		

SEPTEMBER 2023

S	M	T	W	T	F	S
					1	2
3	4	5	6	7	8	9
10	11	12	13	14	15	16
17	18	19	20	21	22	23
24	25	26	27	28	29	30

OCTOBER 2023

S	M	T	W	T	F	S
1	2	3	4	5	6	7
8	9	10	11	12	13	14
15	16	17	18	19	20	21
22	23	24	25	26	27	28
29	30	31				

NOVEMBER 2023

S	M	T	W	T	F	S
			1	2	3	4
5	6	7	8	9	10	11
12	13	14	15	16	17	18
19	20	21	22	23	24	25
26	27	28	29	30		

DECEMBER 2023

S	M	T	W	T	F	S
					1	2
3	4	5	6	7	8	9
10	11	12	13	14	15	16
17	18	19	20	21	22	23
24	25	26	27	28	29	30
31						

HOLIDAYS

The holidays listed in this calendar are accurate to the best of our knowledge and research. All times in this calendar are given in Eastern Standard Time (EST), which is noted as Eastern Daylight Time (EDT) during Daylight Saving Time.

1. Jewish and Bahá'í holidays begin at sundown the evening before the date given.

2. Islamic holidays begin at sundown the evening before the date given. The Islamic calendar is based on lunar observation and thus may vary depending upon the sighting of the crescent moon. Dates apply to North America.

3. Solar and lunar eclipses are not viewable from all regions.

AUGUST 2022
- 1 August Bank Holiday (Scotland)
- 1 Civic Holiday (Canada)
- 1 Lughnasa (Pagan)
- 7 Tisha B'Av (Jewish)[1]
- 8 Ashurah (Islamic)[2]
- 15 Dormition of the Theotokos (Orthodox)
- 29 Summer Bank Holiday (UK)
- 31 Ganesh Chaturthi (Hindu)

SEPTEMBER 2022
- 5 Labor Day (USA, Canada)
- 10 Mid-Autumn Festival (Asian)
- 11 Grandparents Day
- 11 Patriot Day
- 16 Independence Day (Mexico)
- 22 Mabon (Pagan)
- 26 Navaratri begins (Hindu)
- 26 Rosh Hashanah (Jewish New Year)[1]

OCTOBER 2022
- 5 Yom Kippur (Jewish)[1]
- 10 Columbus Day
- 10 Indigenous Peoples Day
- 10 Sukkot begins (Jewish)[1]
- 10 Thanksgiving (Canada)
- 18 Simchat Torah (Jewish)[1]
- 24 Diwali (Hindu)
- 26 Birth of the Báb (Bahá'í)[1]
- 27 Birth of Bahá'u'lláh (Bahá'í)[1]
- 30 British Summer Time ends (UK)
- 31 Halloween
- 31 Samhain (Pagan)

NOVEMBER 2022
- 1 All Saints' Day (Christian)
- 1 Day of the Dead (Mexico)
- 2 All Souls' Day (Christian)
- 6 Daylight Saving Time ends
- 8 Election Day
- 11 Remembrance Day (Australia, Canada, UK)
- 11 Veterans Day
- 24 Thanksgiving
- 27 Advent begins (Christian)
- 30 St. Andrew's Day (Scotland)

DECEMBER 2022
- 8 Bodhi Day (Buddhist)
- 19 Hanukkah begins (Jewish)[1]
- 21 Yule (Pagan)
- 25 Christmas
- 26 Boxing Day (Australia, Canada, UK)
- 26 Kwanzaa begins (African American)
- 31 New Year's Eve

JANUARY 2023
- 1 New Year's Day
- 6 Epiphany (Christian)
- 7 Christmas (Orthodox)
- 16 Martin Luther King Jr. Day
- 22 Chinese New Year (Rabbit)
- 26 Australia Day
- 26 Vasant Panchami (Hindu)

FEBRUARY 2023
- 1 Imbolc (Pagan)
- 2 Groundhog Day
- 6 Tu B'Shevat (Jewish)[1]
- 6 Waitangi Day (New Zealand)
- 14 Valentine's Day
- 15 Flag Day (Canada)
- 15 Nirvana Day (Buddhist)
- 18 Maha Shivaratri (Hindu)
- 20 Presidents' Day
- 21 Losar (Tibetan New Year)
- 21 Mardi Gras
- 22 Ash Wednesday, Lent begins (Christian)
- 27 Great Lent (Orthodox)

MARCH 2023
- 7 Purim (Jewish)[1]
- 8 Holi (Hindu)
- 12 Daylight Saving Time begins
- 17 St. Patrick's Day
- 19 Mother's Day (UK)
- 20 Ostara (Pagan)
- 21 Naw-Rúz (Bahá'í & Persian New Year)
- 23 Ramadan begins (Islamic)[2]
- 26 British Summer Time begins (UK)

APRIL 2023
- 1 April Fools' Day
- 2 Palm Sunday (Christian)
- 6 Passover begins (Jewish)[1]
- 7 Good Friday (Christian)
- 9 Easter (Christian)
- 9 Palm Sunday (Orthodox)
- 10 Easter Monday (Australia, Canada, UK)
- 16 Pascha (Orthodox)
- 18 Yom HaShoah (Jewish)[1]
- 21 Eid al-Fitr (Islamic)[2]
- 22 Earth Day
- 25 ANZAC Day (Australia, New Zealand)
- 27 Freedom Day (South Africa)
- 28 Arbor Day

MAY 2023
- 1 Beltane (Pagan)
- 1 Early May Bank Holiday (UK)
- 1 May Day
- 5 Cinco de Mayo
- 5 Vesak (Buddhist)
- 14 Mother's Day
- 18 Ascension (Christian)
- 22 Victoria Day (Canada)
- 25 Ascension (Orthodox)
- 26 Shavuot (Jewish)[1]
- 28 Pentecost (Christian)
- 29 Ascension of Bahá'u'lláh (Bahá'í)[1]
- 29 Memorial Day
- 29 Spring Bank Holiday (UK)

JUNE 2023
- 4 Pentecost (Orthodox)
- 4 Saka Dawa (Tibetan Buddhist)
- 5 World Environment Day
- 14 Flag Day
- 18 Father's Day
- 21 Juneteenth
- 21 Litha (Pagan)
- 24 St. Jean-Baptiste Day (Quebec)
- 28 Eid al-Adha (Islamic)[2]

JULY 2023
- 1 Canada Day
- 4 Independence Day
- 12 Orangemen's Day (Northern Ireland)
- 14 Bastille Day (France)
- 19 Muharram (Islamic New Year)[2]
- 27 Tisha B'Av (Jewish)[1]
- 28 Ashurah (Islamic)[2]

AUGUST 2023
- 1 Lughnasa (Pagan)
- 7 August Bank Holiday (Scotland)
- 7 Civic Holiday (Canada)
- 15 Dormition of the Theotokos (Orthodox)
- 28 Summer Bank Holiday (UK)

SEPTEMBER 2023
- 4 Labor Day (USA, Canada)
- 10 Grandparents Day
- 11 Patriot Day
- 16 Independence Day (Mexico)
- 16 Rosh Hashanah (Jewish New Year)[1]
- 19 Ganesh Chaturthi (Hindu)
- 23 Mabon (Pagan)
- 25 Yom Kippur (Jewish)[1]
- 29 Mid-Autumn Festival (Asian)
- 30 Sukkot begins (Jewish)[1]

OCTOBER 2023
- 8 Simchat Torah (Jewish)[1]
- 9 Columbus Day
- 9 Indigenous Peoples Day
- 9 Thanksgiving (Canada)
- 15 Navaratri begins (Hindu)
- 16 Birth of the Báb (Bahá'í)[1]
- 17 Birth of Bahá'u'lláh (Bahá'í)[1]
- 29 British Summer Time ends (UK)
- 31 Halloween
- 31 Samhain (Pagan)

NOVEMBER 2023
- 1 All Saints' Day (Christian)
- 1 Day of the Dead (Mexico)
- 2 All Souls' Day (Christian)
- 5 Daylight Saving Time ends
- 7 Election Day
- 11 Remembrance Day (Australia, Canada, UK)
- 11 Veterans Day
- 12 Diwali (Hindu)
- 23 Thanksgiving
- 30 St. Andrew's Day (Scotland)

DECEMBER 2023
- 3 Advent begins (Christian)
- 8 Bodhi Day (Buddhist)
- 8 Hanukkah begins (Jewish)[1]
- 21 Yule (Pagan)
- 25 Christmas
- 26 Boxing Day (Australia, Canada, UK)
- 26 Kwanzaa begins (African American)
- 31 New Year's Eve

AUGUST 2022

SUNDAY	MONDAY	TUESDAY	WEDNESDAY
31	1 August Bank Holiday (Scotland) Civic Holiday (Canada)	2	3
7	8	9	10
14	15	16	17
21	22	23	24
28	29 Summer Bank Holiday (UK)	30	31

● NEW MOON   ◐ FIRST QUARTER   ○ FULL MOON   ◑ LAST QUARTER

THURSDAY	FRIDAY	SATURDAY
4	◑ 7:06 am EDT 5	6
○ 9:36 pm EDT 11	12	13
18	◑ 12:36 am EDT 19	20
25	26	● 4:17 am EDT 27
1	2	3

AUGUST

AUGUST 2022

MONDAY

1

August Bank Holiday (Scotland) | Civic Holiday (Canada) | Lughnasa (Pagan/Wiccan)

TUESDAY

2

WEDNESDAY

3

◑ 7:06 am EDT

Tisha B'Av (Jewish)[1]

AUGUST

AUGUST 2022

MONDAY

8

Ashurah (Islamic)[2]

TUESDAY

9

WEDNESDAY

10

11

○ 9:36 pm EDT

12

13

14

AUGUST 2022

MONDAY

15

Dormition of the Theotokos (Orthodox Christian)

TUESDAY

16

WEDNESDAY

17

FRIDAY

19

◑ 12:36 am EDT

SATURDAY

20

SUNDAY

21

AUGUST

AUGUST 2022

MONDAY
22

TUESDAY
23

WEDNESDAY
24

FRIDAY

26

Women's Equality Day

SATURDAY

27

● 4:17 am EDT

SUNDAY

28

AUGUST 2022

MONDAY
29

Summer Bank Holiday (UK)

TUESDAY
30

WEDNESDAY
31

Ganesh Chaturthi (Hindu)

Our
true home
is in the
here
and now.

Thich Nhat Hanh

SEPTEMBER 2022

SUNDAY	MONDAY	TUESDAY	WEDNESDAY
28	29	30	31
4	5 Labor Day (USA, Canada)	6	7
11	12	13	14
18	19	20	21
● 5:54 pm EDT 25	26 Rosh Hashanah (Jewish New Year)[1]	27	28

● NEW MOON ◐ FIRST QUARTER ○ FULL MOON ◑ LAST QUARTER

THURSDAY	FRIDAY	SATURDAY
1	2	◑ 2:08 pm EDT 3
8	9	○ 5:59 am EDT 10
15	16	◑ 5:52 pm EDT 17
22	23	24
Autumnal Equinox 29	30	1

SEPTEMBER 2022

◑ 2:08 pm EDT

SEPTEMBER 2022

MONDAY

5

Labor Day (USA, Canada)

TUESDAY

6

WEDNESDAY

7

FRIDAY

9

Mercury Retrograde until October 2

SATURDAY

10

Mid-Autumn Festival (Asian) | ○ 5:59 am EDT

SUNDAY

11

Grandparents Day | Patriot Day

SEPTEMBER 2022

MONDAY
12

TUESDAY
13

WEDNESDAY
14

THURSDAY

15

FRIDAY

16

Independence Day (Mexico)

SATURDAY

17

◗ 5:52 pm EDT

SUNDAY

18

SEPTEMBER 2022

MONDAY
19

TUESDAY
20

WEDNESDAY
21

International Day of Peace

Autumnal Equinox 9:04 pm EDT | Mabon (Pagan/Wiccan)

● 5:54 pm EDT

SEPTEMBER 2022

MONDAY

26

Navaratri begins (Hindu) | Rosh Hashanah (Jewish New Year)[1]

TUESDAY

27

WEDNESDAY

28

29

30

OCTOBER 2022

SUNDAY	MONDAY	TUESDAY	WEDNESDAY
25	26	27	28
◑ 8:14 pm EDT 2	3	4	5
			Yom Kippur (Jewish)[1]
○ 4:55 pm EDT 9	10	11	12
	Columbus Day Indigenous Peoples Day Thanksgiving (Canada)		
16	◐ 1:15 pm EDT 17	18	19
23	24	● 6:49 am EDT 25	26
30 British Summer Time ends (UK)	31 Halloween		

● NEW MOON   ◐ FIRST QUARTER   ○ FULL MOON   ◑ LAST QUARTER

29	30	1
6	7	8
13	14	15
20	21	22
27	28	29

OCTOBER

Learning how to
live deeply in each moment
of our daily life
is our true practice.

Thich Nhat Hanh

OCTOBER 2022

SATURDAY

1

SUNDAY

2

◑ 8:14 pm EDT

OCTOBER 2022

TUESDAY
4

WEDNESDAY
5

Yom Kippur (Jewish)[1]

THURSDAY

6

FRIDAY

7

OCTOBER

SATURDAY

8

SUNDAY

9

○ 4:55 pm EDT

OCTOBER 2022

MONDAY

10

Columbus Day | Indigenous Peoples Day | Sukkot begins (Jewish)[1] | Thanksgiving (Canada)

TUESDAY

11

Thich Nhat Hanh's Birthday (1926)

WEDNESDAY

12

13

14

OCTOBER

15

16

OCTOBER 2022

· ·

MONDAY

17

◐ 1:15 pm EDT

· ·

TUESDAY

18

Simchat Torah (Jewish)[1]

· ·

WEDNESDAY

19

· ·

THURSDAY

20

FRIDAY

21

OCTOBER

SATURDAY

22

SUNDAY

23

OCTOBER 2022

Diwali (Hindu) | United Nations Day

Partial Solar Eclipse 7:00 am EDT[3] | ● 6:49 am EDT

Birth of the Báb (Bahá'í)[1]

27

Birth of Bahá'u'lláh (Bahá'í)[1]

28

29

30

British Summer Time ends (UK)

OCTOBER 2022

MONDAY

31

Halloween | Samhain (Pagan/Wiccan)

Don't throw
your suffering
away. Use it.
Your **suffering**
is the compost
that gives you the
understanding
to **nourish**
your happiness
and the **happiness**
of **others.**

Thich Nhat Hanh

NICHOLAS
KIRSTEN
HOSHIN

NOVEMBER 2022

SUNDAY	MONDAY	TUESDAY	WEDNESDAY
30	31	◑ 2:37 am EDT 1	2
6	7	○ 6:02 am EST 8	9
Daylight Saving Time ends		Election Day	
13	14	15	◑ 8:27 am EST 16
20	21	22	● 5:57 pm EST 23
27	28	29	◑ 9:36 am EST 30
			St. Andrew's Day (Scotland)

● NEW MOON   ◑ FIRST QUARTER   ○ FULL MOON   ◑ LAST QUARTER

THURSDAY	FRIDAY	SATURDAY
3	4	5
10	11	12
	Remembrance Day (Australia, Canada, UK) Veterans Day	
17	18	19
24	25	26
Thanksgiving		
1	2	3

855-228
0777
nurses

NOVEMBER 2022

TUESDAY

1

All Saints' Day (Christian) | Day of the Dead (Mexico) | ◑ 2:37 am EDT

WEDNESDAY

2

All Souls' Day (Christian)

Daylight Saving Time ends

MONDAY

7

TUESDAY

8

Election Day | Total Lunar Eclipse 5:59 am EST[3] | ○ 6:02 am EST

WEDNESDAY

9

10

11

Remembrance Day (Australia, Canada, UK) | Veterans Day

12

NOVEMBER

13

MONDAY

14

TUESDAY

15

WEDNESDAY

16

◑ 8:27 am EST

NOVEMBER 2022

● 5:57 pm EST

24

Thanksgiving

25

26

NOVEMBER

27

Advent begins (Christian)

NOVEMBER 2022

MONDAY
28

TUESDAY
29

WEDNESDAY
30

St. Andrew's Day (Scotland) | ◑ 9:36 am EST

Mindfulness
is the **light** that shows us
the way.
It is the living buddha
inside each of us.

Thich Nhat Hanh

NOVEMBER

DECEMBER 2022

SUNDAY	MONDAY	TUESDAY	WEDNESDAY
27	28	29	30
4	5	6	O 11:08 pm EST 7
11	12	13	14
18	19	20	21
	Hanukkah begins (Jewish)[1]		Winter Solstice
25 Christmas	26 Boxing Day (Australia, Canada, UK) Kwanzaa begins (African American)	27	28

● NEW MOON ◐ FIRST QUARTER ○ FULL MOON ◑ LAST QUARTER

THURSDAY	FRIDAY	SATURDAY
1	2	3
8	9	10
15	◗ 3:56 am EST 16	17
22	● 5:17 am EST 23	24
◗ 8:20 pm EST 29	30	31
		New Year's Eve

DECEMBER 2022

FRIDAY

2

SATURDAY

3

SUNDAY

4

DECEMBER 2022

MONDAY
5

TUESDAY
6

WEDNESDAY
7

Pearl Harbor Remembrance Day | ○ 11:08 pm EST

8

Bodhi Day (Buddhist)

9

10

Human Rights Day

11

DECEMBER 2022

MONDAY
12

TUESDAY
13

WEDNESDAY
14

15

FRIDAY

16

◗ 3:56 am EST

SATURDAY

17

SUNDAY

18

DECEMBER 2022

MONDAY

19

_____

_____

_____

_____

Hanukkah begins (Jewish)[1]

TUESDAY

20

_____

_____

_____

_____

WEDNESDAY

21

_____

_____

_____

_____

Winter Solstice 4:48 pm EST | Yule (Pagan/Wiccan)

22

23

● 5:17 am EST

24

25

Christmas

DECEMBER

DECEMBER 2022

MONDAY
26

Boxing Day (Australia, Canada, UK) | Kwanzaa begins (African American)

TUESDAY
27

WEDNESDAY
28

Mercury Retrograde until January 18 | ◐ 8:20 pm EST

Year's Eve

JANUARY 2023

SUNDAY	MONDAY	TUESDAY	WEDNESDAY
1	2	3	4
New Year's Day			
8	9	10	11
15	16	17	18
	Martin Luther King Jr. Day		
22	23	24	25
29	30	31	1

● NEW MOON ◐ FIRST QUARTER ○ FULL MOON ◑ LAST QUARTER

JANUARY

THURSDAY	FRIDAY	SATURDAY
5	○ 6:08 pm EST 6	7
12	13	◑ 9:10 pm EST 14
19	20	● 3:53 pm EST 21
26	27	◐ 10:19 am EST 28
Australia Day		
2	3	4

The practice
of mindfulness
is the practice
of love itself.

Thich Nhat Hanh

SUNDAY

1

New Year's Day

JANUARY 2023

MONDAY
2

TUESDAY
3

WEDNESDAY
4

FRIDAY

6

Epiphany (Christian) | ○ 6:08 pm EST

SATURDAY

7

Christmas (Orthodox Christian)

SUNDAY

8

JANUARY 2023

MONDAY
9

TUESDAY
10

WEDNESDAY
11

12

FRIDAY

13

SATURDAY

14

◑ 9:10 pm EST

SUNDAY

15

JANUARY 2023

- -
MONDAY
16

- -

Martin Luther King Jr. Day | Religious Freedom Day
- -
TUESDAY
17

- -
WEDNESDAY
18

- -

THURSDAY

19

FRIDAY

20

SATURDAY

21

● 3:53 pm EST

SUNDAY

22

Chinese New Year (Rabbit)

JANUARY 2023

MONDAY

23

TUESDAY

24

WEDNESDAY

25

26

Australia Day | Vasant Panchami (Hindu)

27

Holocaust Remembrance Day (International)

28

◑ 10:19 am EST

29

JANUARY 2023

MONDAY
30

TUESDAY
31

Breathing in,
I see myself as space.
Breathing out, I feel free.

Thich Nhat Hanh

JANUARY

FEBRUARY 2023

SUNDAY	MONDAY	TUESDAY	WEDNESDAY
29	30	31	1
○ 1:29 pm EST 5	6	7	8
12	◑ 11:01 am EST 13	14 Valentine's Day	15 Flag Day (Canada)
19	● 2:06 am EST 20 Presidents' Day	21	22 Ash Wednesday, Lent begins (Christian)
26	◑ 3:06 am EST 27	28	1

● NEW MOON   ◑ FIRST QUARTER   ○ FULL MOON   ◐ LAST QUARTER

2	3	4
Groundhog Day		
9	10	11
16	17	18
23	24	25
2	3	4

FEBRUARY

FEBRUARY 2023

WEDNESDAY

1

Imbolc (Pagan/Wiccan)

2

Groundhog Day

3

FEBRUARY

4

5

○ 1:29 pm EST

FEBRUARY 2023

MONDAY

6

Tu B'Shevat (Jewish)¹ | Waitangi Day (New Zealand)

TUESDAY

7

WEDNESDAY

8

THURSDAY
9

FRIDAY
10

FEBRUARY

SATURDAY
11

SUNDAY
12

Lincoln's Birthday (1809)

FEBRUARY 2023

MONDAY

13

◑ 11:01 am EST

TUESDAY

14

Valentine's Day

WEDNESDAY

15

Flag Day (Canada) | Nirvana Day (Buddhist)

16

17

FEBRUARY

Random Acts of Kindness Day

18

Maha Shivaratri (Hindu)

19

FEBRUARY 2023

MONDAY

20

Presidents' Day | ● 2:06 am EST

TUESDAY

21

Losar (Tibetan New Year) | Mardi Gras

WEDNESDAY

22

Ash Wednesday, Lent begins (Christian) | Washington's Birthday (1732)

THURSDAY

23

FRIDAY

24

FEBRUARY

SATURDAY

25

SUNDAY

26

FEBRUARY 2023

MONDAY

27

Great Lent (Orthodox Christian) | ◑ 3:06 am EST

TUESDAY

28

To take care
of ourselves,
we take care
of those
around us.

Thich Nhat Hanh

NICHOLAS
KIRSTEN
HOUSHIN

MARCH 2023

SUNDAY	MONDAY	TUESDAY	WEDNESDAY
26	27	28	1
5	6	○ 7:40 am EST 7	8
12	13	◑ 10:08 pm EDT 14	15
19 Daylight Saving Time begins	20 Spring Equinox	● 1:23 pm EDT 21	22
26 British Summer Time begins (UK)	27	◐ 10:32 pm EDT 28	29

● NEW MOON ◐ FIRST QUARTER ○ FULL MOON ◑ LAST QUARTER

THURSDAY	FRIDAY	SATURDAY
2	3	4
9	10	11
16	17	18
23 St. Patrick's Day	24	25
30 Ramadan begins (Islamic)[2]	31	1

MARCH

MARCH 2023

WEDNESDAY

1

MARCH

MARCH 2023

MONDAY

6

TUESDAY

7

Purim (Jewish)[1] | ○ 7:40 am EST

WEDNESDAY

8

Holi (Hindu) | International Women's Day

MARCH

Daylight Saving Time begins

MARCH 2023

MONDAY

13

TUESDAY

14

◐ 10:08 pm EDT

WEDNESDAY

15

St. Patrick's Day

MARCH

Mother's Day (UK)

MARCH 2023

· ·

MONDAY

20

_____

_____

_____

_____

Ostara (Pagan/Wiccan) | Spring Equinox 5:25 pm EDT
· ·

TUESDAY

21

_____

_____

_____

_____

Naw-Ruz (Bahá'í & Persian New Year) | ● 1:23 pm EDT
· ·

WEDNESDAY

22

_____

_____

_____

_____

_____

· ·

23

Ramadan begins (Islamic)[2]

24

25

MARCH

26

British Summer Time begins (UK)

MARCH 2023

MONDAY
27

TUESDAY
28

◗ 10:32 pm EDT

WEDNESDAY
29

APRIL 2023

SUNDAY	MONDAY	TUESDAY	WEDNESDAY
26	27	28	29
2	3	4	5
9	10	11	12
Easter (Christian)	Easter Monday (Australia, Canada, UK)		
16	17	18	19
23	24	25	26
30		ANZAC Day (Australia, New Zealand)	

● NEW MOON ◐ FIRST QUARTER ○ FULL MOON ◑ LAST QUARTER

THURSDAY	FRIDAY	SATURDAY
30	31	1
		April Fools' Day
○ 12:34 am EDT 6	7	8
Passover begins (Jewish)[1]	Good Friday (Christian)	
◑ 5:11 am EDT 13	14	15
● 12:12 am EDT 20	21	22
	Eid al-Fitr (Islamic)[2]	Earth Day
◔ 5:20 pm EDT 27	28	29

The mind can go
in a **thousand directions**.
But on this beautiful path,
I walk in peace.
With **each step**, a flower blooms.

Thich Nhat Hanh

APRIL 2023

SATURDAY

1

April Fools' Day

SUNDAY

2

APRIL

Palm Sunday (Christian)

APRIL 2023

MONDAY

3

TUESDAY

4

WEDNESDAY

5

· ·

THURSDAY

6

_____

_____

_____

_____

_____

_____

Passover begins (Jewish)[1] | ○ 12:34 am EDT
· ·

FRIDAY

7

_____

_____

_____

_____

Good Friday (Christian)
· ·

SATURDAY

8

_____

_____

_____

_____

_____

_____

· ·

SUNDAY

9

_____

_____

_____

_____

_____

Easter (Christian) | Palm Sunday (Orthodox Christian)
· ·

APRIL

APRIL 2023

MONDAY

10

Easter Monday (Australia, Canada, UK)

TUESDAY

11

WEDNESDAY

12

13

◗ 5:11 am EDT

14

15

16

Pascha (Orthodox Christian)

APRIL

APRIL 2023

MONDAY
17

TUESDAY
18

Tax Day | Yom HaShoah (Jewish)[1]

WEDNESDAY
19

20

Hybrid Solar Eclipse 12:17 am EDT[3] | ● 12:12 am EDT

21

Eid al-Fitr (Islamic)[2] | Mercury Retrograde until May 14

22

Earth Day

23

APRIL

APRIL 2023

MONDAY
24

TUESDAY
25

ANZAC Day (Australia, New Zealand)

WEDNESDAY
26

Freedom Day (South Africa) | ◑ 5:20 pm EDT

FRIDAY

28

Arbor Day

SATURDAY

29

SUNDAY

30

MAY 2023

SUNDAY	MONDAY	TUESDAY	WEDNESDAY
30	1	2	3
	Early May Bank Holiday (UK)		
7	8	9	10
14	15	16	17
Mother's Day			
21	22	23	24
	Victoria Day (Canada)		
28	29	30	31
	Memorial Day Spring Bank Holiday (UK)		

● NEW MOON ◗ FIRST QUARTER ○ FULL MOON ◑ LAST QUARTER

THURSDAY	FRIDAY	SATURDAY
4	○ 1:34 pm EDT 5	6
11	◑ 10:28 am EDT 12	13
18	● 11:53 am EDT 19	20
25	26 ◐ 11:22 am EDT 27	
1	2	3

MAY 2023

MONDAY
1

Beltane (Pagan/Wiccan) | Early May Bank Holiday (UK) | May Day

TUESDAY
2

WEDNESDAY
3

Cinco de Mayo | Vesak (Buddhist) | Penumbral Lunar Eclipse 1:23 pm EDT[3] | ○ 1:34 pm EDT

MAY 2023

MONDAY

8

_____

TUESDAY

9

_____

WEDNESDAY

10

_____

◑ 10:28 am EDT

Mother's Day

MAY 2023

MONDAY
15

TUESDAY
16

WEDNESDAY
17

18

Ascension (Christian)

19

Bike to Work Day | ● 11:53 am EDT

20

Armed Forces Day

21

MAY 2023

MONDAY

22

Victoria Day (Canada)

TUESDAY

23

WEDNESDAY

24

THURSDAY

25

Ascension (Orthodox Christian)

FRIDAY

26

Shavuot (Jewish)[1]

SATURDAY

27

◑ 11:22 am EDT

SUNDAY

28

Pentecost (Christian)

MAY 2023

Ascension of Bahá'u'lláh (Bahá'í)[1] | Memorial Day | Spring Bank Holiday (UK)

Looking **deeply** at any **one** **thing,** we see the **whole** **cosmos.** The **one** is made of the **many.**

Thich Nhat Hanh

NICHOLAS
KIRSTEN
HOUSHIN

JUNE 2023

SUNDAY	MONDAY	TUESDAY	WEDNESDAY
28	29	30	31
4	5	6	7
11	12	13	14 Flag Day
● 12:37 am EDT 18 Father's Day	19 Juneteenth	20	21 Summer Solstice
25	◑ 3:50 am EDT 26	27	28 Eid al-Adha (Islamic)²

● NEW MOON   ◐ FIRST QUARTER   ○ FULL MOON   ◑ LAST QUARTER

1

2

○ 11:42 pm EDT 3

8

9

◐ 3:31 pm EDT 10

15

16

17

22

23

24

29

30

JUNE

JUNE 2023

FRIDAY

2

JUNE

SATURDAY

3

○ 11:42 pm EDT

SUNDAY

4

Pentecost (Orthodox Christian) | Saka Dawa (Tibetan Buddhist)

JUNE 2023

MONDAY

5

World Environment Day

TUESDAY

6

WEDNESDAY

7

JUNE

◑ 3:31 pm EDT

JUNE 2023

MONDAY
12

TUESDAY
13

WEDNESDAY
14

Flag Day

FRIDAY

16

SATURDAY

17

SUNDAY

18

Father's Day | ● 12:37 am EDT

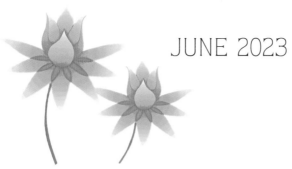

JUNE 2023

MONDAY

19

Juneteenth

TUESDAY

20

World Refugee Day

WEDNESDAY

21

Litha (Pagan/Wiccan) | Summer Solstice 10:58 am EDT

22

23

JUNE

24

St. Jean-Baptiste Day (Quebec)

25

JUNE 2023

MONDAY

26

◑ 3:50 am EDT

TUESDAY

27

WEDNESDAY

28

Eid al-Adha (Islamic)[2]

JULY 2023

SUNDAY	MONDAY	TUESDAY	WEDNESDAY
25	26	27	28
2	○ 7:39 am EDT 3	4	5
		Independence Day	
◑ 9:48 pm EDT 9	10	11	12
			Orangemen's Day (Northern Ireland)
16	● 2:32 pm EDT 17	18	19
			Muharram (Islamic New Year)[2]
23	24	◐ 6:07 pm EDT 25	26
30	31		

● NEW MOON ◐ FIRST QUARTER ○ FULL MOON ◑ LAST QUARTER

29	30	1
		Canada Day
6	7	8
13	14	15
20	21	22
27	28	29

JULY

In order to **understand** others,
we must **know** them
and be inside their skin.
Then we can treat them with
loving kindness.

Thich Nhat Hanh

JULY 2023

SATURDAY

1

Canada Day

SUNDAY

2

JULY 2023

MONDAY

3

○ 7:39 am EDT

TUESDAY

4

Independence Day

WEDNESDAY

5

Dalai Lama's Birthday (1935)

JULY

◗ 9:48 pm EDT

JULY 2023

MONDAY
10

TUESDAY
11

WEDNESDAY
12

Orangemen's Day (Northern Ireland)

THURSDAY

13

FRIDAY

14

Bastille Day (France)

SATURDAY

15

JULY

SUNDAY

16

JULY 2023

MONDAY

17

● 2:32 pm EDT

TUESDAY

18

WEDNESDAY

19

Muharram (Islamic New Year)[2]

JULY

JULY 2023

MONDAY
24

TUESDAY
25

◐ 6:07 pm EDT

WEDNESDAY
26

• •

Tisha B'Av (Jewish)[1]

• •

Ashurah (Islamic)[2]

• •

• •

• •

JULY 2023

MONDAY

31

Breathing in,
I am
still water.
I reflect
the sky
faithfully.

Thich Nhat Hanh

NICHOLAS
KIRSTEN
HONSHIN

AUGUST 2023

SUNDAY	MONDAY	TUESDAY	WEDNESDAY
30	31	○ 2:31 pm EDT 1	2
6	7 August Bank Holiday (Scotland) Civic Holiday (Canada)	◑ 6:28 am EDT 8	9
13	14	15	● 5:38 am EDT 16
20	21	22	23
27	28 Summer Bank Holiday (UK)	29	○ 9:35 pm EDT (Blue Moon) 30

● NEW MOON   ◐ FIRST QUARTER   ○ FULL MOON   ◑ LAST QUARTER

THURSDAY	FRIDAY	SATURDAY
3	4	5
10	11	12
17	18	19
◑ 5:57 am EDT 24	25	26
31	1	

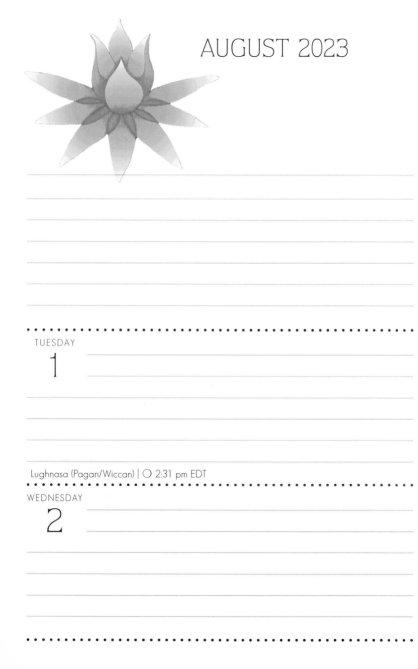

AUGUST 2023

TUESDAY

1

Lughnasa (Pagan/Wiccan) | ○ 2:31 pm EDT

WEDNESDAY

2

AUGUST 2023

MONDAY

7

August Bank Holiday (Scotland) | Civic Holiday (Canada)

TUESDAY

8

◑ 6:28 am EDT

WEDNESDAY

9

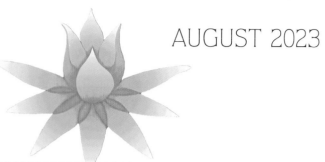

AUGUST 2023

MONDAY
14

TUESDAY
15

Dormition of the Theotokos (Orthodox Christian)

WEDNESDAY
16

● 5:38 am EDT

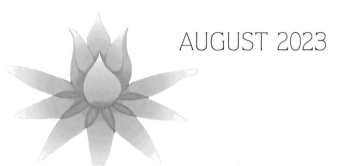

AUGUST 2023

MONDAY
21

TUESDAY
22

WEDNESDAY
23

Mercury Retrograde until September 15

◗ 5:57 am EDT

FRIDAY
25

SATURDAY
26

Women's Equality Day

SUNDAY
27

AUGUST

AUGUST 2023

MONDAY

28

Summer Bank Holiday (UK)

TUESDAY

29

WEDNESDAY

30

○ 9:35 pm EDT (Blue Moon)

SEPTEMBER 2023

SUNDAY	MONDAY	TUESDAY	WEDNESDAY
27	28	29	30
3	4 Labor Day (USA, Canada)	5	◖ 6:21 pm EDT 6
10	11	12	13
17	18	19	20
24	25 Yom Kippur (Jewish)¹	26	27

● NEW MOON   ◐ FIRST QUARTER   ○ FULL MOON   ◑ LAST QUARTER

THURSDAY	FRIDAY	SATURDAY
31	1	2
7	8	9
● 9:40 pm EDT 14	15	16
		Rosh Hashanah (Jewish New Year)[1]
21	◑ 3:32 pm EDT 22	23
		Autumnal Equinox
28	○ 5:57 am EDT 29	30

When we change
our daily lives—
the way we think, speak, and act—
we change the world.

Thich Nhat Hanh

NICHOLAS
KIRSTEN
HONSHIN

SEPTEMBER 2023

FRIDAY
1

SATURDAY
2

SUNDAY
3

SEPTEMBER 2023

MONDAY

4

Labor Day (USA, Canada)

TUESDAY

5

WEDNESDAY

6

◑ 6:21 pm EDT

THURSDAY

7

FRIDAY

8

SATURDAY

9

SUNDAY

10

Grandparents Day

MONDAY

11

Patriot Day

TUESDAY

12

WEDNESDAY

13

THURSDAY
14

● 9:40 pm EDT

FRIDAY
15

SATURDAY
16

Independence Day (Mexico) | Rosh Hashanah (Jewish New Year)[1]

SUNDAY
17

SEPTEMBER 2023

MONDAY

18

TUESDAY

19

Ganesh Chaturthi (Hindu)

WEDNESDAY

20

SEPTEMBER

THURSDAY
21

International Day of Peace

FRIDAY
22

◐ 3:32 pm EDT

SATURDAY
23

Autumnal Equinox 2:50 am EDT | Mabon (Pagan/Wiccan)

SUNDAY
24

MONDAY

25

Yom Kippur (Jewish)[1]

TUESDAY

26

WEDNESDAY

27

28

29

Mid-Autumn Festival (Asian) | ○ 5:57 am EDT

30

Sukkot begins (Jewish)[1]

OCTOBER 2023

SUNDAY	MONDAY	TUESDAY	WEDNESDAY
1	2	3	4
8 Simchat Torah (Jewish)[1]	9 Columbus Day Indigenous Peoples Day Thanksgiving (Canada)	10	11
15	16	17	18
22	23	24	25
29 British Summer Time ends (UK)	30	31 Halloween	1

● NEW MOON ◐ FIRST QUARTER ○ FULL MOON ◑ LAST QUARTER

THURSDAY	FRIDAY	SATURDAY
5	◑ 9:48 am EDT 6	7
12	13	● 1:55 pm EDT 14
19	20	◐ 11:29 pm EDT 21
26	27	○ 4:24 pm EDT 28
2	3	4

OCTOBER

My **actions** are
my only true belongings.
I cannot escape
the **consequences** of my actions.
My actions are the ground
on which **I stand.**

Thich Nhat Hanh

SUNDAY

1

OCTOBER 2023

MONDAY

2

TUESDAY

3

WEDNESDAY

4

5

6

OCTOBER

◑ 9:48 am EDT

7

8

Simchat Torah (Jewish)[1]

OCTOBER 2023

MONDAY

9

Columbus Day | Indigenous Peoples Day | Thanksgiving (Canada)

TUESDAY

10

WEDNESDAY

11

Thich Nhat Hanh's Birthday (1926)

12

13

OCTOBER

14

Annular Solar Eclipse 1:59 pm EDT[3] | ● 1:55 pm EDT

15

Navaratri begins (Hindu)

OCTOBER 2023

MONDAY
16

Birth of the Báb (Bahá'í)[1]

TUESDAY
17

Birth of Bahá'u'lláh (Bahá'í)[1]

WEDNESDAY
18

THURSDAY

19

FRIDAY

20

OCTOBER

SATURDAY

21

◐ 11:29 pm EDT

SUNDAY

22

MONDAY

23

TUESDAY

24

United Nations Day

WEDNESDAY

25

Partial Lunar Eclipse 4:14 pm EDT[3] | ○ 4:24 pm EDT

British Summer Time ends (UK)

OCTOBER 2023

MONDAY

30

TUESDAY

31

Halloween | Samhain (Pagan/Wiccan)

To **practice** looking deeply is the **basic medicine** for anger, hatred, and fear.

Thich Nhat Hanh

NOVEMBER 2023

SUNDAY	MONDAY	TUESDAY	WEDNESDAY
29	30	31	1
◑ 3:37 am EST 5 Daylight Saving Time ends	6	7 Election Day	8
12	● 4:27 am EST 13	14	15
19	◐ 5:50 am EST 20	21	22
26	○ 4:16 am EST 27	28	29

 ● NEW MOON ◐ FIRST QUARTER ○ FULL MOON ◑ LAST QUARTER

THURSDAY	FRIDAY	SATURDAY
2	3	4
9	10	11 Remembrance Day (Australia, Canada, UK) Veterans Day
16	17	18
23	24	25
Thanksgiving		
30	1	2
St. Andrew's Day (Scotland)		

NOVEMBER

NOVEMBER 2023

WEDNESDAY

1

All Saints' Day (Christian) | Day of the Dead (Mexico)

All Souls' Day (Christian)

NOVEMBER

Daylight Saving Time ends | ◑ 3:37 am EST

NOVEMBER 2023

MONDAY

6

TUESDAY

7

Election Day

WEDNESDAY

8

THURSDAY

9

FRIDAY

10

SATURDAY

11

NOVEMBER

Remembrance Day (Australia, Canada, UK) | Veterans Day

SUNDAY

12

Diwali (Hindu)

NOVEMBER 2023

MONDAY

13

● 4:27 am EST

TUESDAY

14

WEDNESDAY

15

THURSDAY

16

FRIDAY

17

SATURDAY

18

SUNDAY

19

NOVEMBER 2023

MONDAY
20

● 5:50 am EST

TUESDAY
21

WEDNESDAY
22

23

Thanksgiving

24

25

NOVEMBER

26

NOVEMBER 2023

MONDAY
27

○ 4:16 am EST

TUESDAY
28

WEDNESDAY
29

St. Andrew's Day (Scotland)

DECEMBER 2023

SUNDAY	MONDAY	TUESDAY	WEDNESDAY
26	27	28	29
3	4	◐ 12:49 am EST 5	6
10	11	● 6:32 pm EST 12	13
17	18	◑ 1:39 pm EST 19	20
24	25	○ 7:33 pm EST 26	27
31 New Year's Eve	Christmas	Boxing Day (Australia, Canada, UK) Kwanzaa begins (African American)	

● NEW MOON   ◐ FIRST QUARTER   ○ FULL MOON   ◑ LAST QUARTER

THURSDAY	FRIDAY	SATURDAY
30	1	2
7	8	9
	Hanukkah begins (Jewish)¹	
14	15	16
21	22	23
Winter Solstice		
28	29	30

The only thing **worthy** of **you** is **compassion**—invincible, limitless, **unconditional**.

Thich Nhat Hanh

DECEMBER 2023

FRIDAY
1

SATURDAY
2

SUNDAY
3

Advent begins (Christian)

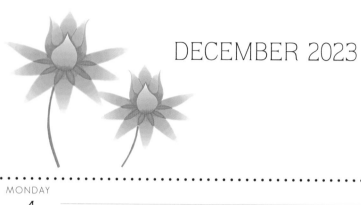

DECEMBER 2023

MONDAY

4

TUESDAY

5

◑ 12:49 am EST

WEDNESDAY

6

THURSDAY

7

Pearl Harbor Remembrance Day

FRIDAY

8

Bodhi Day (Buddhist) | Hanukkah begins (Jewish)[1]

SATURDAY

9

SUNDAY

10

DECEMBER

Human Rights Day

DECEMBER 2023

MONDAY

11

TUESDAY

12

● 6:32 pm EST

WEDNESDAY

13

Mercury Retrograde until January 1

THURSDAY
14

FRIDAY
15

SATURDAY
16

SUNDAY
17

DECEMBER

DECEMBER 2023

MONDAY

18

TUESDAY

19

◑ 1:39 pm EST

WEDNESDAY

20

Winter Solstice 10:28 pm EST | Yule (Pagan/Wiccan)

DECEMBER 2023

MONDAY

25

Christmas

TUESDAY

26

Boxing Day (Australia, Canada, UK) | Kwanzaa begins (African American) | ○ 7:33 pm EST

WEDNESDAY

27

THURSDAY

28

FRIDAY

29

SATURDAY

30

SUNDAY

31

DECEMBER

New Year's Eve

JANUARY 2024

SUNDAY	MONDAY	TUESDAY	WEDNESDAY
31	1	2	◑ 10:30 pm EST 3
	New Year's Day		
7	8	9	10
14	15	16	◑ 10:53 pm EST 17
	Martin Luther King Jr. Day		
21	22	23	24
28	29	30	31

● NEW MOON ◐ FIRST QUARTER ○ FULL MOON ◑ LAST QUARTER

THURSDAY	FRIDAY	SATURDAY
4	5	6
● 6:57 am EST 11	12	13
18	19	20
○ 12:54 pm EST 25	26	27
1	Australia Day 2	3

BIRTHDAYS AND OCCASIONS

....

_____

_____

_____

_____

_____

_____

....

January _____ February _____

_____ _____

_____ _____

_____ _____

_____ _____

_____ _____

....

March _____ April _____

_____ _____

_____ _____

_____ _____

_____ _____

_____ _____

....

May _____ June _____

_____ _____

_____ _____

_____ _____

_____ _____

_____ _____

....

BIRTHDAYS AND OCCASIONS

July

August

September

October

November

December

Our true home is in the here and now.

Quote: Thich Nhat Hanh, *A Rose for Your Pocket*, Parallax Press
Artwork: *The Eternal Lovers – Two Becoming One
through Unconditional Love* (detail)
© Nicholas Kirsten-Honshin

Learning how to live deeply in each moment
of our daily life is our true practice.

Quote: Thich Nhat Hanh, *Reconciliation*, Parallax Press
Artwork: *Brother Raven Bringing the Golden Moment Home*
© Nicholas Kirsten-Honshin

Don't throw your suffering away. Use it.
Your suffering is the compost that gives you
the understanding to nourish your happiness
and the happiness of others.

Quote: Thich Nhat Hanh, *Fidelity*, Parallax Press
Artwork: *Flowers of the Sun Bringing Light to Winter's Heart*
© Nicholas Kirsten-Honshin

Mindfulness is the light that shows us the way.
It is the living buddha inside each of us.

Quote: Thich Nhat Hanh, *Touching Peace*, Parallax Press
Artwork: *Offering to the Angel of Peace* © Nicholas Kirsten-Honshin

The practice of mindfulness is the practice of love itself.

Quote: Thich Nhat Hanh, *Touching Peace*, Parallax Press
Artwork: *Butterfly Contemplating Transformation and Rebirth
of the Golden Moments* © Nicholas Kirsten-Honshin

Breathing in, I see myself as space.
Breathing out, I feel free.

Quote: Thich Nhat Hanh, *Touching Peace*, Parallax Press
Artwork: *Mystic Messenger* © Nicholas Kirsten-Honshin

To take care of ourselves,
we take care of those around us.

Quote: Thich Nhat Hanh, *Cultivating the Mind of Love*, Parallax Press
Artwork: *An Offering of Blossoms of Compassion and Love*
© Nicholas Kirsten-Honshin

The mind can go in a thousand directions.
But on this beautiful path, I walk in peace.
With each step, a flower blooms.

Quote: Thich Nhat Hanh,
Present Moment Wonderful Moment, Parallax Press
Artwork: *Flowers of the Compassionate Heart* © Nicholas Kirsten-Honshin

Looking deeply at any one thing,
we see the whole cosmos.
The one is made of the many.

Quote: Thich Nhat Hanh, *Cultivating the Mind of Love*, Parallax Press
Artwork: *Forget Me Not* © Nicholas Kirsten-Honshin

In order to understand others,
we must know them and be inside their skin.
Then we can treat them with loving kindness.

Quote: Thich Nhat Hanh, *Happiness*, Parallax Press
Artwork: *Ladybug Experiencing the Golden Moments
of Peace and Joy* © Nicholas Kirsten-Honshin

Breathing in, I am still water.
I reflect the sky faithfully.

Quote: Thich Nhat Hanh, *Call Me by My True Names*, Parallax Press
Artwork: *Healing Compassion Emanates through
Moon Mountain Lake and Flower* © Nicholas Kirsten-Honshin

When we change our daily lives—the way we think,
speak, and act—we change the world.

Quote: Thich Nhat Hanh, *The World We Have*, Parallax Press
Artwork: *Healing Journey of the Ascending Spirit* (detail)
© Nicholas Kirsten-Honshin

My actions are my only true belongings.
I cannot escape the consequences of my actions.
My actions are the ground on which I stand.

Quote: Thich Nhat Hanh, *Reconciliation*, Parallax Press
Artwork: *Sacred Spirit Tree* © Nicholas Kirsten-Honshin

To practice looking deeply is the basic medicine
for anger, hatred, and fear.

Quote: Thich Nhat Hanh, *How to See*, Parallax Press
Artwork: *You Can Find Heaven, Even in a Bunch of Green Onions*
© Nicholas Kirsten-Honshin

The only thing worthy of you is compassion—
invincible, limitless, unconditional.

Quote: Thich Nhat Hanh, *Call Me by My True Names*, Parallax Press
Artwork: *Ascending Lotus* © Nicholas Kirsten-Honshin

2024 AT A GLANCE

JANUARY 2024

S	M	T	W	T	F	S
	1	2	3	4	5	6
7	8	9	10	11	12	13
14	15	16	17	18	19	20
21	22	23	24	25	26	27
28	29	30	31			

FEBRUARY 2024

S	M	T	W	T	F	S
				1	2	3
4	5	6	7	8	9	10
11	12	13	14	15	16	17
18	19	20	21	22	23	24
25	26	27	28	29		

MARCH 2024

S	M	T	W	T	F	S
					1	2
3	4	5	6	7	8	9
10	11	12	13	14	15	16
17	18	19	20	21	22	23
24	25	26	27	28	29	30
31						

APRIL 2024

S	M	T	W	T	F	S
	1	2	3	4	5	6
7	8	9	10	11	12	13
14	15	16	17	18	19	20
21	22	23	24	25	26	27
28	29	30				

MAY 2024

S	M	T	W	T	F	S
			1	2	3	4
5	6	7	8	9	10	11
12	13	14	15	16	17	18
19	20	21	22	23	24	25
26	27	28	29	30	31	

JUNE 2024

S	M	T	W	T	F	S
						1
2	3	4	5	6	7	8
9	10	11	12	13	14	15
16	17	18	19	20	21	22
23	24	25	26	27	28	29
30						

JULY 2024

S	M	T	W	T	F	S
	1	2	3	4	5	6
7	8	9	10	11	12	13
14	15	16	17	18	19	20
21	22	23	24	25	26	27
28	29	30	31			

AUGUST 2024

S	M	T	W	T	F	S
				1	2	3
4	5	6	7	8	9	10
11	12	13	14	15	16	17
18	19	20	21	22	23	24
25	26	27	28	29	30	31

SEPTEMBER 2024

S	M	T	W	T	F	S
1	2	3	4	5	6	7
8	9	10	11	12	13	14
15	16	17	18	19	20	21
22	23	24	25	26	27	28
29	30					

OCTOBER 2024

S	M	T	W	T	F	S
		1	2	3	4	5
6	7	8	9	10	11	12
13	14	15	16	17	18	19
20	21	22	23	24	25	26
27	28	29	30	31		

NOVEMBER 2024

S	M	T	W	T	F	S
					1	2
3	4	5	6	7	8	9
10	11	12	13	14	15	16
17	18	19	20	21	22	23
24	25	26	27	28	29	30

DECEMBER 2024

S	M	T	W	T	F	S
1	2	3	4	5	6	7
8	9	10	11	12	13	14
15	16	17	18	19	20	21
22	23	24	25	26	27	28
29	30	31				